FOXES

First published in Great Britain in 1991 by
Colin Baxter Photography Ltd.,
Unit 2/3, Block 6,
Caldwellside Industrial Estate,
LANARK, ML11 6SR

British Library Cataloguing in Publication Data
Graham, Keith
    Foxes
    I. Canidae
    I. Title
    599.74442

    ISBN 0-948661-20-8

Photographs by

Front Cover © George Bernard (Oxford Scientific Films)
Back Cover © Mick Chesworth (Aquila)
Page 19 © Wendy Shattill/Bob Rozinski
Page 20 © Hans Reinhard (Bruce Coleman)
Page 21 © Leonard Lee Rue III (Frank Lane)
Page 22 © Jane Burton (Bruce Coleman)
Page 23 © George Bernard (Oxford Scientific Films)
Page 24 © George Bernard (Oxford Scientific Films)
Page 25 © Mick Chesworth (Aquila)
Page 26 © Nellaine Price (Survival Anglia)
Page 27 © Leonard Lee Rue III (Frank Lane)
Page 28 © Silverstris (Frank Lane)
Page 29 © George Bernard (Oxford Scientific Films)

Page 30 © John Lunch (Survival Anglia)
Page 35 © Hans Reinhard (Bruce Coleman)
Page 36 © Leonard Lee Rue III (Frank Lane)
Page 37 © M. Wilding (Survival Anglia)
Page 38 © George Bernard (Oxford Scientific Films)
Page 39 © Colin Baxter
Page 40 © Leonard Lee Rue III (Frank Lane)
Page 41 © Leonard Lee Rue III (Frank Lane)
Page 42 © A. R. Hamblin (ARPS) (Frank Lane)
Page 43 © R. T. Mills (Aquila)
Page 44 © Keith Graham
Page 45 © Hans Reinhard (Bruce Coleman)
Page 46 © R. Glover (Aquila)

Fox Illustration © Keith Brockie

Printed in Great Britain by
Frank Peters (Printers) Ltd., Kendal.

FOXES

Keith Graham

Colin Baxter Photography Ltd., Lanark, Scotland

Foxes

A thick blanket of freezing fog enveloped the fields of a dark December evening, not the ideal conditions for a walk, but dogs have to be exercised and so there was nothing else for it but to wrap up and venture out . . . albeit reluctantly.

The grass crunched crisply beneath my booted feet as we groped our way across the big field, the beam from my torch penetrating no further than three or four yards. We seemed to be surrounded by glistening grey walls of nothingness.

The hair poking out from beneath my cap was already sodden and stiffening in the freezing conditions. Then, without warning, I was literally frozen to the spot – transfixed – by the unearthly sound of a blood-curdling scream that had the hairs on the back of my neck bristling. I wheeled round but the light from my torch simply rebounded from the walls of impenetrable grey . . . providing only enough illumination for me to realise that my canine companion was also bristling like a hedgehog.

Now I heard the padding of delicate feet in the hoar. From her initial position directly behind us, the vixen began to describe a circle. Again, from no more than a few yards away to our right, that same unearthly scream echoed from the thick, crystaline blanket . . . and again, as she now advanced to a position dead ahead. From our left and then, once more, from directly behind us, that devilish wail was repeated, each voiceless interval permeated only by the relentless, measured tread of her feet in the frost.

She circled us once more, before, in response to a distant and muffled triple bark, she uttered one more scream and in a flurry of footsteps was gone!

That was my first really close encounter with a fox, yet that dancing, screaming dervish had been completely invisible to me on such a visionless night. Perhaps she knew that the dull senses of mere mortals pale into insignificance compared with her own honed sense of smell and her keen hearing which told all she wanted to know about who and what was about in her frozen garden of Eden.

Since then I have enjoyed many other close encounters with red foxes. I have come to respect them and I hope I have come to know them. I have also found that the complexity of the lifestyle of foxes, whether in the hunting countryside of Leicestershire where that first blind date took place, in the rock-strewn hills of the Lake District, or in both the highlands and the lowlands of Scotland, has had for me an absolutely fatal attraction.

The fox is either a hero or a villain. To generations of countryfolk, Tod, as he is known in the north, has always been a villain, prone to make mincemeat of poultry and lambs, a killer of awesome prowess, a sneak thief who gets up to all manner of crafty and underhand tricks in order to win a meal. Yet, ironically, as the fox has increasingly invaded the urban areas of Britain, another, more benign attitude has developed in the minds of townsfolk, many of whom delight in the spectacle of foxes padding through their gardens or sunning themselves on walls or flat-topped roofs, and even rearing their young under potting-sheds and garages.

And it is interesting to reflect that in those urban situations, foxes are, without question, of benefit to mankind. As they patrol the leafy gardens of suburbia, or the remnants of old industrial estates and docklands, they act as unpaid pest-control officers. Rats, mice and voles are their principal sources of food even if they have also developed a remarkable instinct for tracking down extra dietary items from dustbins, sometimes scattering the contents far and wide as each item is picked over for its culinary quality. In fact, it might be said, in this context, that foxes generally confine themselves to the better parts of town where richer pickings can be obtained. They are not, it seems, so keen on the remains of Chinese take-aways, much preferring the fatty off-cuts from the Sunday joint discarded by an ever more fastidious public, and the vast quantities of surplus food regularly discarded by our increasingly affluent society.

However, there are those charged with the responsibility of controlling any outbreak of rabies in this country should it occur, who inevitably view the swelling population of foxes in urban areas with deep apprehension and suspicion. Statistical evidence from the other side of the Channel confirms that the fox is the most likely vector in spreading rabies. However, on the bright side of that menacing picture, is the success experienced in attracting foxes to baits containing an anti-rabies vaccine; results in various parts of Europe suggest that this deadly disease can perhaps be at least partly controlled in this way.

The red fox *(Vulpes vulpes)* is distributed right across the northern hemisphere. It is commonplace throughout Europe and Asia from the Arctic regions to the Indian sub-continent. But the red fox is also present in America and Australia. In the latter case, its presence is very much due to the introduction of the animal from Britain, probably in the middle of the last century, as a hunting quarry. The same may or may not be true of its American presence. Certainly, when America was a British colony, it is known that foxes were shipped out from Britain. However, there is some confusion due to the presence of a very similar species, the cross fox *(Vulpes fulva)*, which some experts believe to be the same species as our red fox in spite of the markings along the spine and across the shoulders which gives the species its common name.

Since the isolation of Britain after the Ice Age, it might be presumed that the native British fox has been typecast, so to speak, and has consequently become a specific sub-species. However, the picture has been confused by the repeated introduction of foxes from the Continent and Scandinavia. All these importations were, it seems, designed to satisfy the demands of the fox-hunting fraternity which suggests that natural fox numbers were not really sufficient to fulfil the needs of the emerging hunts of the eighteenth and nineteenth centuries. Indeed, this piece of factual history may be responsible for the apparent differences between the 'greyhound foxes' of highland Scotland and the perceptibly smaller foxes of the British lowlands. Many experts suggest that the highland fox is really descended from the Scandinavian fox. Certainly it is generally bigger, longer in the leg and has an obviously larger skull. However, many other factors may have contributed to these apparent differences: habitat, food, and not least, separate development in relative isolation without the influence of foreign imports.

That foxes have always been a target for huntsmen there can be no doubt, but the evidence does seem to suggest that foxes were not high on the list of preferences for the Normans who, perhaps more than anyone, enjoyed such sports and did much to introduce them to these shores. Rather, deer and hares were very much more popular quarries, perhaps because in addition to the thrill of the chase, they at least also provided food. Yet foxes have historically been hunted as a means to an end here and elsewhere – firstly by early man, who no doubt used their pelts for clothing, and later by warreners whose responsibilities included the defence of their rabbit charges, then so much in demand as food, by both man and beast. Much later, foxes became animals of the chase, the objects of 'sport'.

Fox hunting is an ancient sport dating back thousands of years, yet a sport generally perceived to be reserved for the pleasure of the 'upper classes'. The real growth of fox hunting as we know it in Britain, came in the eighteenth and nineteenth centuries, no doubt popularised even more by the 'nouveaux riches' who were able to ride to hounds on the back of the wealth they had accumulated from the wheels of early industry. Brian Vesey-Fitzgerald, in his *Town Fox, Country Fox,* reveals that during the mid-nineteenth century, a thousand foxes a year were sold annually at Leadenham market in Lincolnshire, all of which were released into the English countryside in order to provide the hunters with their sport. If such is a measure of the fox population in England at that time, then it must be assumed that foxes were not at all commonplace. Such evidence rather dilutes suggestions made by masters of foxhounds, that their purpose always has been and still is, to control foxes. I know from my own brief sojourn in Leicestershire during the 1960s, that cubs were still being hand-reared for later release. Oscar Wilde described fox hunting in its most traditional form – on horseback – as the activity of the unspeakable in pursuit of the uneatable! There is, of course, another dimension to fox hunting, notably in the Lake District, where the sport is pursued on foot rather than on horseback. Such hunts, supported vigorously by many hill sheep farmers have, arguably, a much sounder base for their existence, for small hill lambs are obviously vulnerable, especially during their first few days of life, to predation by foxes.

It may be presumed that the aforementioned importations actually introduced new genetic pools and that may, in some measure, account for the variations frequently reported in the size and coloration of foxes. As a general rule of thumb guide, the average red fox measures about 42 inches (107cm) from the tip of its nose to the tip of its tail. It is, by the way, a fallacy that the dog has a white tip to the tail and the vixen does not. The majority of foxes, male and female, have a white-tipped tail. An average fox may weigh 12-15 lbs (6.5kg) and its coat is notoriously red. However, when it comes to colour there are many subtle variations on a theme. Some are more yellow, some browner, some quite grey. Close examination of the coat of a fox reveals russet, grey, black, white, dark brown and almost yellow hairs, which, in varying distribution may partially account for the apparent colour differences. The underparts of most foxes range from a dirty white to a blueish grey and almost all foxes have black lower limbs and black on the back of their ears. On rare occasions, black underparts have also been recorded in British foxes, perhaps a throw-back to early imports.

All species of fox have particular and readily identified hallmarks. Most obviously, they are dog-like creatures, the main physical features of which are the often caricatured pointed muzzle, large erect ears and the characteristically bushy tail. Our red fox is the largest of them all; the smallest being the Fennec fox of the North African deserts, a real lightweight of just $3^{1}/2$ lbs (1.5kg). Perhaps the most distinctive is the Arctic fox with its white coat. There are, however, two colour phases – white and 'blue'. Elsewhere in the world, over twenty different species of fox have been identified.

The tail, or 'brush', is a particularly familiar physical feature and, in hunting country, symbolic of the 'kill'. In areas where fox clubs exist, a bounty is still paid to gamekeepers on the production of each brush, outside traditional hunting country of course. Farmers and sporting estate managers are the main subscribers to such clubs. In hunting country, the destruction of foxes by gamekeepers is rather infra dig!

Near the base of the tail is a dark spot beneath which is a scent gland. However, the fox also 'scents' through urine, the anal gland and through its feet; hence the scent trail left by a fox pursued by hounds. It is said that the longer the chase, the fainter the scent given off by the pads.

The ammonia-like scent emitted by foxes represents their calling card . . . perhaps even their identification card in a sense and is a significant means of communication in the private lives of these fascinating animals. It is, of course, also a means of marking territorial boundaries, sometimes buried food caches and often, a means of marking members of the same group. Foxes frequently scent upon each other.

The tracks of foxes are sometimes difficult to discern from those of dogs but a really good print in soft ground reveals that the toes have hairs between them. The configuration is more or less diamond-shaped with the triangular pad surmounted by four toes. Often the claw marks can be discerned and the trail is familiarly straight, each footstep following the others, more or less in line astern. The home of a fox is called either a den or earth. Often, old rabbit burrows are enlarged and sometimes unoccupied sections of extensive badger setts are used. Indeed, there are many accounts of fox and badger cubs playing together. Foxes are, however, eminently capable of excavating their own dens and are accomplished diggers. In urban locations, foxes show remarkable ingenuity, taking over derelict buildings, invading basements and particularly favouring such places as abandoned railway track embankments.

Other signs of fox presence, apart from the obvious scenting, are the frequent placement of droppings, usually on prominent tufts of grass, stones or fallen logs. Fox droppings are generally dark, almost black, long and twisted with tapered ends.

Fox droppings tell their own tales. They certainly provide a remarkably accurate indication of each individual fox's diet. In most cases, the dominant materials contained in the 'scats' are the indigestible bones and claws of small mammals or the scaly remains of insects which, together, probably form the bulk of the fox's food.

In particular, short-tailed field voles may account for an exceptionally high proportion of the diet, especially in the uplands and most especially in sheep farming country where the vole population is much higher than most people might suspect. However, it is impossible to generalise, for the fox is, without doubt, a very adaptable creature when it comes to food. Worms, beetles and other invertebrates, birds, rabbits, fruits, grass and other vegetable matter are all consumed with relish. So too, many farmers will tell you, are lambs and poultry!

Perhaps this is the key to the success of foxes; that they can adapt to almost any kind of habitat . . . and earn a reasonable living from the widest possible choice of food. Hence have I watched foxes high up on a highland mountain, in the fields and woodlands of the lowlands, amongst the sand dunes of the coast, in suburbia and in industrial estates. I have observed foxes 'roosting' in trees and on one occasion, watched one pad a good half-mile across the frozen waters of a loch to investigate a deserted wildfowl roost.

Each of the twenty-one different species of fox which have been identified throughout the world, has its own special adaptations and food preferences but the red fox seems to be particularly versatile.

Unlike their fairly close relations, wolves, foxes do not live in large communities or packs. That is not to say that they are solitary animals. They do live in social groups, yet for all our familiarity with them, we do not, I believe, fully understand their lifestyle.

Territory size inevitably depends upon the terrain – and of course, upon the food resources that are to be found in a particular patch. Territory size will also inevitably fluctuate, influenced by the movement of itinerant foxes and by the activities of man. However, in the mountain areas of highland Scotland, for instance, territories will be correspondingly larger than is likely to be the case in better provisioned lowland areas. Some probably run to several thousand hectares, whereas in more productive areas they may dwindle to as little as ten. Each territory is established by a dog fox but of course, his claims will, over the weeks, months and years, be constantly challenged by other dogs.

Sharing each territory will be a group of vixens, generally numbering three or four. They do not usually live together but they do keep in constant contact, leaving their 'calling cards' – scent and droppings – and, from time to time, communicating vocally. Perhaps the most familiar of the fox-voices is the spine-chilling, long-drawn-out scream – as I heard on that freezing, foggy night. This is generally thought to be more commonly uttered by the vixens although dog foxes do sometimes scream. The other most familiar vocalisation manifests itself in barking – usually three or four rapidly repeated staccato barks.

Voice contact of this kind may be explained, for the most part, as simply a method of communication within social groups and even between neighbouring communities. But at the turn of the year, when the vixens come into season, these vocal exchanges have a good deal more significance. Close meetings between foxes can also produce a high-pitched and quite gutteral explosion of noise . . . a continuous volley of yelps, sometimes ending in a submissive and even higher-pitched whine. Cubs playing can be very noisy indeed and high-pitched yelping and chattering is very much a sound-feature of family fox-earths.

Foxes also exhibit a fascinating vocabulary of body language. When two foxes meet, there is often a display of body movement and vocalisation which might be compared with the shaking of hands or the bowing which are a part of man's body language patterns. There is, typically, the submissive gesture in which the ears are laid back, the mouth opened in a kind of grin. Often the body is arched, and if the two are of equal standing, they often line up sideways and barge into each other, tails looped, pushing with their flanks. This pattern of behaviour is often accompanied by high-pitched whining and 'gekkering' – a term used by David Macdonald in his comprehensive work on foxes, *Running with the Fox*, which accurately describes the sound emanating from such a confrontation. If one is dominant, the other will approach with its body low to the ground, mouth gaping, tail lashing, sometimes rolling over on to its back in complete submission. Two equals may also indulge in bouts of 'wrestling', during which each animal rears up on its hind legs, front paws placed on the other's shoulders. Typically, in such encounters, mouths gape wide open and the ears are laid back. Usually one will gain the ascendancy – if only marginally – in which case the other will demur and subsequently submit to its superior. An aggressive fox acts in much the same way as a dog, ears pricked forward, tail raised. Foxes do fight, sometimes furiously but, as is nearly always the case in nature, most pecking orders are worked out without recourse to serious physical combat – a simple expedient which is commonplace throughout nature because serious injuries sustained in battle do not contribute to long-term survival. It is more usually a case of mind over matter, the stronger-willed emerging as the more dominant.

In the main, a dog fox will only mate with one of the vixens in his territory. Each year, the vixens contest a position of dominance and it is the dominant vixen in a group which thereafter becomes responsible for producing the next generation of that family of foxes. However, such is fox-society that sometimes the other vixens will act as 'nursemaids', helping in the general rearing and care of the cubs. The same vixen may not hold the dominant position from year to year.

Recent research shows that there is, in the breeding behaviour, a safeguard designed to sustain numbers. This applies particularly in areas where foxes are vigorously harassed or in urban situations where fox populations may suffer from above average road casualties. In such circumstances, the dog fox may be stimulated to mate with more than one of his vixens. This may have some relevance in the area of fox control – an emotive and often oversimplified subject.

The vixen is only receptive for about three days, and once mating has taken place, gestation is approximately fifty-two days. The average litter generally numbers four or five. However, much larger litters have frequently been recorded. Much must inevitably depend upon habitat and food supply.

The cubs are not at all fox-like when first born. They are most often chocolate brown – sometimes almost black – and their ears are small and rounded, as is the case in newborn kittens or puppies. Their eyes open at about ten days and they may make their first appearance above ground usually at about four weeks of age.

It is during these first few weeks of their lives that they are at their most vulnerable. 'Cubbing', when fox hunters seek out dens or earths, send in their terriers and kill the cubs – and the vixen if she does not eventually bolt – is a well-practised activity. But the vixen may well be alert to such threats and will, if she suspects that her underground nursery is threatened, move her cubs quickly to an alternative home, carrying each one in turn by the scruff of the neck.

During these first few weeks, it is generally the duty of the dog fox to supply the vixen and her cubs with food. Often he is not even allowed to enter the earth at all during this period, the vixen meeting him to collect food supplies, presumably at some pre-arranged tryst.

If an earth is discovered by the hunters and the cubs eliminated, and possibly the vixen too, the dog will sometimes continue to bring food to the usual meeting place. I have often heard it said that if his mate has been killed and thus fails to pick up the 'drop', the dog will react by bringing ever increasing quantities of food; a reaction not easy to explain.

Play is an important factor in the lives of young mammals, especially in young carnivores. Badgers play with an astonishing degree of vigour and noise. Fox-cubs, too, appear to devote an amazing amount of energy and time to playing, although in my personal experience, they are not quite as noisy and are generally that little bit more wary than young badgers, ready to dive earthwards at the first sign of apparent danger, often signalled by the attendant vixen. This is all part of a learning process designed to equip them for survival.

In a litter, a pattern of dominance will often emerge which will probably carry through into adult life. A dominant cub will presumably always command a more prominent part in the general order of things; perhaps this demonstrates the truth of 'the survival of the fittest'. But there are also little nuances to learn. During these early days, the vixen is extremely attentive, not only suckling and cleaning her offspring fastidiously, but actually encouraging play by flicking her brush to stimulate her cubs to pounce and catch it.

The youngsters will also play with feathers, with the bodies of small mammals and with insects, perhaps chasing beetles. And they will also play with inanimate objects in much the same way as do kittens. Tugs of war will occur over food scraps . . . then they resemble puppies. Even scraps of grass, blown on the wind, will attract attention. Soon they are learning to 'stalk' such objects. A fox earth is readily distinguished from a badger sett by the litter and food remains around it; badgers would not tolerate such untidiness!

Throughout this vital learning period, the cubs are honing the instinctive assets with which they are naturally equipped, their almost extrasensory sense of smell and their keen hearing. Their ears by now are shaping up, becoming proportionately larger and pointed. Eyesight is the least sensitive of a fox's senses, at its best at close quarters. Like all mammals, foxes live in a monochrome world and have no sense of colour. But do not imagine that foxes have poor eyesight. Black and white – or more likely grey – it may be, but movement is perhaps the key, and a memory for familiar forms and silhouettes. The pupils of the fox eye are elliptical in shape and react in much the same way as the eyes of cats, reducing to vertical slits in bright light. However, it would, I believe, be a mistake to underrate the eyesight of foxes.

For the first twelve weeks of their lives, they will stick pretty close to the vixen, learning from her the skills of hunting and survival, learning smells and sounds which may spell danger, on the one hand, or sources of food on the other. At this stage they begin to explore the immediate surrounds of the earth independently, although they are not as yet, by any means, self-sufficient. That complete independence will come soon enough for the dog cubs, although the vixens may be cushioned somewhat, by being allowed to remain in the parents' territory for a little longer, or even permanently sometimes.

Meanwhile, the vixen will not bring as much food to the earth but may leave it some distance away, or even hide it – another lesson for the cubs. The brighter cubs will be the first to find the hidden food and they will, inevitably, be the most successful survivors.

It is worth remembering, that apart from in the eagle country of highland Scotland, fox cubs have no other enemy but man. Eagles, as Mike Tomkies, that extra-ordinary highland explorer, has recorded, will freely take fox cubs as food for their own young. But man poses the main threat, and the cubs must learn to be very wary of *Homo sapiens* in these first formative months. The average life span of a fox is probably no more than three years although, in captivity or man-free environments, foxes can reach ages of thirteen or fourteen, roughly the same life span as a dog.

As the autumn comes, young dog foxes in particular, must carve out their own niches in life. Inevitably, they will find it hard to become established in territories close to their home base unless all the dog foxes in neighbouring landscapes have not survived the predation of man. They sometimes travel very considerable distances in an effort to find permanent bases, and even then it may take a year or more. These, then, are the 'travelling people' of fox society and probably the most vulnerable section of the fox population.

It is during the first few months of their lives that foxes are most at risk. Man has devised many ways of trapping foxes. Some have been outlawed . . . yet are sometimes still used. The gin-trap was, for many long years, one of the principal means of catching foxes, often in 'drowning traps' designed to drag the victim into pools of water. There are many savage stories of foxes having been thus caught, escaping by biting off the trapped limb. Today's principal weapon against the fox is the locking snare – now the only legal snare – set usually on regular fox routes. Like most mammals, foxes are creatures of habit and often use the same 'highways' time and time again. The most obvious places for snare settings are along fence lines.

The present law demands that anyone setting snares must examine them every twenty-four hours. Some fox trappers claim that the snare is a relatively humane way of trapping foxes. However, this might be questioned. I have seen dead or dying foxes thus ensnared and been well aware that the creatures had suffered a lingering, choking death. The other problem with snares, of course, is that they cannot, and do not, discriminate between foxes and other animals. Badgers are frequently trapped and killed in snares, as are cats. And deer, too, can be caught by the legs. In fact any mammal of the right size is vulnerable and that, of course, includes dogs.

Where it is necessary to control foxes, shooting is probably the most effective way. There have been moves afoot to ban snares altogether but there is a hidden danger. Recent press reports have highlighted the problems caused by the strictly illegal practice of setting poisoned baits. However, there are those who persist in using poison as a weapon against both foxes and crows. The publicity has come from the discovery of birds of prey, most usually buzzards, which have died after feeding upon poisoned baits. Eagles have similarly perished as have kites. In Scotland, which has been bereft of red kites for over a hundred years, these once common raptors have been re-introduced by the Nature Conservancy Council and the Royal Society for the Protection of Birds. One of the earliest of these releases was found dead at such a bait, most commonly presented in the shape of a rabbit, sliced open and laced with a poison such as alpha-chlorolose; buzzards, kites and eagles, eager to exploit carrion food sources, are particularly susceptible. Heavy fines have been administered in recent years and it is hoped that such practices will eventually be eliminated.

The damage done by foxes is a contentious issue. Visit hill sheep farming country and you will be assailed by any number of horrific stories which recount the dastardly deeds of foxes and their predation upon lambs. Foxes kill lambs, let there be no doubt. But how many viable lambs do they kill? I have never seen a fox kill a lamb in spite of the fact that I have spent a good deal of time watching foxes in hill sheep country. A hill sheep-farmer of my acquaintance, with a lifetime of out-and-out war against foxes under his belt – he attended his first 'kill' when he was nine years old – recently admitted to me that, in his sixty-two years, he has only ever seen a fox kill a lamb once. But such a dramatic revelation comes as no surprise. By and large, Tod works under the cover of darkness, and who is out and about on the high hills at such times? Nevertheless, a hill sheep-farmer or a shepherd, discovering a trail of dead lambs on his first morning round is not easy to console . . . and not too well-disposed towards foxes.

Extensive research into the predation of foxes upon lambs born to hill sheep has been conducted. None of these research projects however, so far as I know, have ever revealed a kill in excess of four per cent of the lambs born on a 'hard' hill. The most recent, conducted by Dr Ray Hewson of the Department of Zoology at the University of Aberdeen, concentrated on an estate in the far north-west of Scotland upon which fox control of any kind was suspended for a period of three years. During that time, the survey showed no increase in lamb mortality. Similar work carried out by Dr Hewson in Argyll, also pertinently revealed that lamb mortality on the Morvern Peninsular and nearby Mull, were exactly the same. There are, by reputation, extremely active fox populations in Morvern, and no foxes at all on Mull.

Such statistics, of course, do not appease hill farmers who find lambs killed by foxes or who find dens in which the remains of lambs are left. The stories are legion, but the real evidence is relatively scant. How many lamb carcases found at an earth, or, for that matter, in an eagle eyrie, were dead when they were taken? And how many of the victims would, in any case, have perished due to any number of causes? How many were weak and abandoned? Lamb mortality in the highlands is inevitably high. Most hill sheep in highland Scotland drop their lambs towards the end of April and into early May, at a time when the vagaries of the weather are renowned. Sudden blizzards and, more appositely, wild, wet and windy conditions can be very hard on lambing hill sheep, taking condition off the ewes very rapidly and, as a result, curtailing the milk supply to their lambs.

Today, the management of hill sheep flocks is much less intensive than it once was. There is not, for instance, the manpower in the hills that there was even a few decades ago. The number of lambing ewes under the charge of a shepherd is, these days, far higher than it was when extensive sheep farming was introduced to the highlands some two hundred years ago. This change has been forced by sheer economics.

Lambs die for any number of reasons – disease, the birth of twins which may mean that a poorly conditioned ewe has only enough milk to feed just one of her offspring, a lack of adequate feeding, the inexperience of gimmers (first lambers); separation from the ewe at an early age through natural or unnatural causes. Lamb losses in hard country can easily top thirty per cent in an average year and much more in a really bad spring.

And, there are foxes! However, in my personal experience, no predator will work unnecessarily hard to find food. A dead or dying lamb or any form of carrion, for that matter, is the easiest source of food for a parent fox, far easier to acquire than a mobile live lamb unless it has been deserted by the ewe. On the high hills, fox cubs are born in the month of April, coinciding with the arrival of lambs. The ewe after-birth, incidentally, seems to be a particularly favoured food of suckling vixens. There is also evidence of super intelligence in some dog foxes. I have even heard of a dog fox, whose mate had been killed whilst the cubs were suckling, deliberately slaughtering young lambs primarily for the milk contained in their stomachs.

And many hill farmers of my acquaintance regret bitterly the absence of rabbits from their glens. The deliberate introduction of myxomatosis in the 1950s, might well have saved tons of lowland crops but in hill country, it may be regretted, having stripped many areas of a natural and relatively easily obtained source of fox food. The arrival of extensive modern forests in the upland areas has also made a contribution to the fox problem. Many hill farmers claim that the forests provide shelter for foxes and other predators. More significant may be the loss of suitable habitat for the small mammals – notably voles – which results as a forest matures. And voles, as I have said, are probably the single most important food item for hill foxes.

In its initial stages, a forest provides ideal conditions for voles and many predators, but once the trees begin to mature and cover the ground, the natural vegetation, and consequently, the vole population, decline steeply.

Predator populations run parallel to the availability of food. If there is plenty of food for short-eared owls, kestrels, stoats, weasels and foxes, for instance, their populations will grow accordingly. The decline is sharp once a forest begins to mature and the choices facing the predators are either to move on to pastures new or to find other sources of food.

The fox on the left probably represents the archetypal image of 'Tod',
broad head (this is probably a dog), long, narrow snout and
slanted eyes. Yet there is, in reality, no archetype. The
specimen above is, by contrast, more dog-like
and exhibits a longer, silkier coat.

Fox cubs, at birth, are very dark, sometimes almost black. Their eyes do not
open until they are about ten days old. The vixen is a dedicated mother
and the cubs develop quickly. By about four weeks of age they are
already taking their first faltering steps towards the outside world.

After initial caution, the cubs are soon exploring the immediate environs of
the den, playing with each other and with scraps of food or
inanimate objects. They are naturally inquisitive – all part
of the vital early period of education for survival.

By the time they are eight weeks old, the cubs are becoming increasingly
adventurous. As part of the educational process, the vixen may
sometimes hide or bury food at short distances from the
earth. But, at this stage, the earth still provides security.

At three months of age, fox cubs are becoming increasingly independent,
often indulging in solo explorations. The adventurous cub on the right,
shows off the cat-like nature of the fox's eyes – elliptical in shape.

Man versus Fox

Whichever way you look at it, man's management of the landscape has a far-reaching impact on all other living things. It does not seem unreasonable to suppose that the introduction of extensive sheep farming just over two hundred years ago, especially in highland Scotland, altered the balance. Duncan Ban McIntyre, the Gaelic poet from Glen Orchy, bemoaned the arrival of sheep on his favourite hill, Beinn Dorain; "My blessings with the foxes dwell, for that they hunt the sheep so well. Ill f'a the sheep, a grey faced nation; that swept our hills with desolation . . .", implying that the sheep were destroying the scrub-filled and wooded hill landscape of his youth . . . and that the foxes might indirectly wreak appropriate revenge.

It is easy to get caught up with the fox/lamb issue and, in my experience, there are certainly more complaints about fox predation during a poor spring when natural mortality is high. But the fact remains that there are many instances of quite serious losses of lambs to foxes, mostly, it seems, during the first week of their lives. Hill sheepfarming has become a precarious business with ever increasing threats to the subsidies which have not only kept hill farming going but which have also maintained working communities in the uplands. It is therefore easy to understand why the fox is identified as an enemy – along with all the other hazards. Nonetheless, the evidence points to the destruction of cubs in the earth as the only really effective method of keeping a population in check, and the winter killing of foxes may be extremely counter-productive, perhaps stimulating extra breeding vigour in the fox population.

The picture in the lowlands is a little more confused. There are no longer flocks of farmyard poultry for Tod to attack. Most of our poultry these days is lucky indeed ever to see proper daylight. They are kept almost exclusively in intensive and artificially lit environments. As David Stephen, that great Scottish naturalist once remarked, "I've never yet found a fox carrying a key to get into the hen house!"

It is, nevertheless, when the subject of foxes and poultry arises that Tod is most frequently accused of wanton killing. It is true that if a fox does gain access to a poultry house, it will often go on the rampage and slaughter many of the occupants. Such deeds evoke comments such as, ". . . killing for killing's sake!" However, in such circumstances, the predator is acting instinctively. Panicking hens produce a natural stimulus in the fox to chase and kill. Given the unlikely scenario in which a poultry keeper was then to leave the carcases where they were, it is distinctly likely that the fox might return in order to remove at least some of the surplus to a suitable cache. I have lost plenty of hens and ducks to foxes and on one occasion put the theory to the test. The fox returned the following night and duly removed more of its victims.

Lowland sheep are also much less vulnerable to fox predation. They lamb early in the year long before most foxes have cubbed, and these days, more and more of them are being lambed indoors.

Another contentious issue is, of course, game. Pheasant shooting has grown in popularity. Vast sums of money are expended in breeding and raising pheasants for the shoot. And, here again, a food source has been introduced into the environment which was not originally there. Of course foxes prey upon pheasants, but by and large, it may be fair to say that only young and semi-wild sitting hen pheasants are really vulnerable.

It is when the question of fox control is addressed that the real enigmas emerge. It is estimated that some 50,000 foxes are killed each year in Britain. This massive slaughter does not, however, seem to be making any impression on the overall fox population.

Some are shot; even more probably are snared. But it is worth remembering that every time a fox is killed, it leaves a vacancy for others which may be seized upon not just by a single fox but by more than one. Furthermore, David Macdonald in his lifelong study of foxes reveals the stark fact that where fox populations are unduly harassed, the breeding rate increases to compensate.

There is a parallel to be struck with the Ministry of Agriculture's abortive attempts to clear badgers from parts of south-west England in relation to the spread of Bovine TB. In affected areas, badger setts were systematically gassed and their occupants killed. It was, however, discovered that after an interval of time the gassed setts were re-occupied by surplus neighbouring populations and consequently had to be assaulted again.

Macdonald's work on urban foxes, who, as I have said, are more vulnerable to traffic accidents, reveals that dog foxes, under such pressures, will mate with more than one vixen. It is simply nature's way of protecting the species. Does the moral to be drawn from such evidence point to the fact that the more foxes you kill, the more will fill the empty spaces and thus that this is a war without logical end? Certainly it is the view of many who, without sentiment and equipped with nothing more than experience, some technology in the form of radio tracking, hours of careful observation and pragmatism, believe that the time, money and effort spent in trying to control foxes is not economically justifiable.

The subject of the hunt is even more emotive and on occasions moves people to violence. The anti-hunt lobby has undoubtedly gained in strength. But emotion can often cloud judgement. Anyone who cares about animals, one would think, is bound to have a feeling of revulsion at the spectacle of a pack of hounds tearing a pursued fox to pieces. Yet those who follow the hunt adore their horses and their hounds . . . all of which seems to fly in the face of reason.

In truth, fox hunting, as it is depicted in prints (and on Christmas cards!) is perhaps the least effective way of controlling foxes. The stories of the ability of hunted foxes to evade their pursuers are legion and sometimes hard to believe. It is commonly said that a pursued fox will deliberately lead a hunt into another fox's territory and that a hunt may therefore find itself chasing an endless succession of fresh foxes. I can believe that, for the fox is an intelligent creature. A fox thus hounded will run through water to erase its trail; it will run through a field of livestock in order to confuse the hounds with the scents of many other animals; it will run along the top of a wall, double back along its own trail or even hide up a tree. These are simply the tactics of survival.

Of course, the stories do not stop there. The fox, according to some, will enter water carrying a hollow reed through which to breath, completely submerge itself and thus rid itself of parasites, notably fleas. A fox will also uncork the prickly defences of a hedgehog by rolling it into water, thus forcing it to uncurl and swim for its life, and then launch an underwater attack on the now vulnerable urchin. Such stories are again legion.

Folklore, legends, myths, cartoons and fairy stories have all faithfully adhered to an image which always shows a remarkable degree of cunning, cleverness and intelligence in Reynard the fox. People are even described as 'foxy' or as 'that old fox'.

The fox is all of these things. The fox is also a beautiful creature, a fast mover when there is a need – at the maximum, capable of moving across short distances at over thirty miles an hour – a patient stalker at times displaying feline movement as it slinks forward, body hugging the ground, but seen at its best perhaps, when hunting small mammals. Then, the fox sits patiently on its haunches, ears pricked attentively forward, every nerve taut and ready to spring . . . and then arcs into the air to arrive with its front paws trapping its hapless rodent victim. The fox in such a mode is even more cat-like than the average cat.

And now that the fox has firmly established itself in the suburbs of all our cities, it has become, for most urban people, not an animal to be feared but a creature to admire . . . and a creature in either town or country, which certainly cannot be ignored.

The night's all tremors; my unborn lamb stirs.
I smell fox and in the sky a light beyond understanding.
Stay close, Shepherd.

(Jim Crumley)

An exceptionally keen sense of smell and very sharply honed hearing are
the fox's main assets, allied to a natural stealth and intelligence.
However, when necessary, foxes can move at speed
to a maximum of about 35 mph.

It is in hill sheep-farming country that conflict between man and
fox is at its sharpest. The killing of lambs by foxes is often
overstated but hill lambs are undoubtedly vulnerable to
fox predation during the first week of their lives.

Foxes are generally more active by night than by day, often lying up during
the hours of daylight. But when conditions are hard, hunger drives
them to seek food by both night and day. Intelligent though
foxes are, they cannot identify the trail of potential prey
by sight – for instance, in snow. Scent is the key.

A fox yawning and showing off a fine array of teeth – all 42 of them. Although they are carnivores, foxes are very adaptable when it comes to food. A diet of small mammals and birds, insects and carrion, may often be supplemented by fruit and berries.

Few creatures are as adaptable as foxes. Equally at home in the gentle English
countryside, by the seashore or on a Scottish or Welsh mountain,
foxes seem able to succeed in almost any environment – as
long as there is somewhere to lie up and rest.

Towns and cities have been increasingly infiltrated by foxes.
Suburban dwellers are often treated to the sight of a fox, either padding quietly
through a garden or even resting on a coal bunker in the winter sunshine!
Admired in suburbia yet relentlessly pursued in the countryside, foxes,
above all, are fascinating animals which cannot be ignored.

Fox Watching

With so many foxes now taking up residence in urban areas, your own kitchen or living room window may, ironically, turn out to be the best places from which to watch them. Town foxes have, to some extent, become remarkably bold and some can even be coaxed to come very close to houses and even people, when regular food offerings are made. To my certain knowledge, one group of foxes regularly joins the night shift of an industrial complex in Central Scotland, where the workers share their sandwiches with them.

Foxes, as have been pointed out repeatedly, are exceptionally adaptable. And with the possibility that the total British population may peak at a million shortly after the cubbing season, wherever you are, in town or country, there is every chance of seeing foxes, even if it is only a glimpse of an animal streaking across the road in front of you at dusk.

To watch any animal properly requires some detective work. First find either a den or more profitably a regular fox trail. Foxes like most mammals are creatures of habit and frequently use the same routes. The give-away traces of hairs, perhaps caught on a fence which foxes regularly climb through or under and, if the under-foot conditions are right, the distinctive straight tracks of foxes will tell you where they regularly commune. Then you will have to apply common sense and ensure you stay down-wind, relatively still and silent.

Den watching is usually only feasible during the Spring and early part of Summer, but be warned, should the vixen detect the merest hint of your presence, she will remove herself and the cubs to an alternative location – post haste.

The Red Fox

Latin name - *Vulpes vulpes.*
Order *Canidae.*

Dimensions - Length of head & body - average approximately 2 feet (61cm). Tail - 16-18 inches (40cm).

Weight - Dog: average 15 lbs (6.8kgs).
Vixen: 12 lbs (5.4kgs).

Breeding - Sexual maturity at about ten months. Dog fox, spermatogenesis between November and February. Mating period between end of December and late February. Oestrus in the vixen lasts for three days and occurs correspondingly later in the northern parts of Britain.

Gestation about 52 days. Litter size 4-5.

Distribution - Throughout the Northern Hemisphere - Red foxes are found in North America as far north as Ellesmere Island, to the north-west of Greenland and well within the Arctic Circle and as far south as Mexico. They are widely distributed throughout Europe and Asia, from Ireland in the west to the Bering Sea in the east and from the Arctic regions of Russia and Scandinavia in the north to the Indian sub-continent and the Mediterranean in the south. Red foxes are also present in North Africa, where they survive in desert conditions. They are widespread in Australia, although their presence there is entirely due to man. They may be seen high up in the mountainous regions or, equally, in the streets of our cities.

Biographical Note

Naturalist, writer and broadcaster, Keith Graham has enjoyed a life-long love affair with wildlife. The piecing together of the intricate jigsaw of nature, trying to understand the balances, the innate inter-dependence which is the essence of natural life, has become a fatal fascination for him. He knows that nature can be red in tooth and claw, but that man too is an essential part of the equation. His experiences as a countryside ranger has provided him with many close encounters with birds and animals of all kinds, especially foxes, and he has reared several of them over the years at his Perthshire home.

Recommended Reading

Running with the Fox by David Macdonald, published by Unwin Hyman Ltd., 1987.
Wild Fox by Roger Burroughs, published by David and Charles (Publishers) Ltd., 1968.
Town Fox, Country Fox by Brian Vesey-Fitzgerald, published by Andre Deutsch Ltd., 1967.
Wild Animals of the British Isles by Maurice Burton, D.Sc., published by Frederick Warne & Co Ltd., 1968.
Victim of Myth – a report written and researched by Dr Ray Hewson, M.Sc., Ph.D., M.I.Biol., published for the League Against Cruel Sports by the Department of Zoology, University of Aberdeen, 1990.